The Power Chair

Derilyn Sparrow

The Power Chair

Copyright © 2017 Derilyn Sparrow

All rights reserved under all Copyright Conventions.

Book Cover design by Alexa Sponaugle

Photograph of the author: Kimberly English

ISBN-13: 978-1-979953-01-6
ISBN-10: 1-979953-01-5

Contents

Dedication

This book is dedicated to Sheryl Davis-Colston. Thank you for motivating me daily to follow my dreams. Breakthroughs8 is operational today because you helped me keep the vision alive.

Acknowledgements

To my husband, Robert Sparrow, thank you for motivating and inspiring me to accomplish my lifelong dreams. You have been my rock and my true love. I cherish our life together and look forward to the years ahead that God wants to prosper and bless us.

To my son, Kalvin Williams, who is the reason I wake up every day of my life with purpose. I respect your never-failing encouragement and relentless critiques throughout this project. I respect your opinion. You were a gift from God and I treasure you.

My niece, Alena Smith, is the first person I shared my vision and ideas for Breakthroughs8 with years ago. Her unique perspective and thoughtful critiques were a breath of fresh air. She's talented and a force to be reckoned with. She's my heart.

Alexa Sponaugle, who is like a daughter to me, is a rare gem. She is wise beyond her years with imaginative and innovative creativity. An original mastermind who is gifted in various areas of life and business. I want to personally thank you for the dedication and hard work you gave from the heart. I cherish you more than words can say.

To Kimberly English, who has traveled this awesome journey of Breakthroughs8 with me every day. You are my business partner and trusted friend. You are the perfect blend of intellect and skill; without you, this book would not have been written. Your generosity and tenaciousness are the cornerstone of our success. Thanks for everything.

·1·

Keys to Success

The taste of success is as American as apple pie. There is no shortage of individuals who want to be successful, and every person can obtain it if they're willing to work hard for it. It doesn't matter your environment, socioeconomic situation or ethnicity, you can become whatever you want to be if you are willing to put the effort, persistence, and patience into your dreams. You will not get there through sitting and wait for success to locate you. You must be willing to do whatever it takes to grab it. One of the major mistakes that a person makes is underestimating the amount of time and effort it takes to make it. In a society where most individuals want the glamorous life in a matter of days or months, it's no wonder how disappointing it can be to realize that it takes much more.

The good news is, you can obtain everything that you desire if you focus on what's most important, along with the journey to success. Eight great steps are golden, and if you can complete them with discipline and motivation, you will be on your way.

1

Step 1: Dream it.

Every dream begins in the mind and heart. It can be a fresh idea or one that was previously packaged. It doesn't matter if it's something that you've been thinking about for 8 years or more; pick it up, dust it off, and breathe life back into it. This is something that can change your life and your family forever for the better. Your dream can have an exceptional impact on the world at large. Dream it, believe it and achieve it!

Step 2: Write it.

This step might seem like one you can skip, but don't be tempted to omit it. Writing the vision and your plan of action is paramount to your future success. You can always refer to it when you get stuck along the way. You can also use it to articulate your plan when it comes time for funding or getting others to believe in it. After writing your vision, continue to perfect it along the way as things change. Address any issues and make revisions when needed.

Step 3: Expose it.

Most dreams fall into the abyss because individuals hover over them. One of the worst things to do is become so afraid to share your dream or feel that you alone can accomplish it. Sharing your dream can help others to remind you of it even when you place it on the backburner. Exposure can help you believe in your ability to complete it when it gets tough along the way. Tell any and everyone who will listen. If you encounter negative feedback, use it to get better or decide to reject it.

2

Step 4: Envision it.

Go to a store, sit in an executive chair and vision yourself owning it. Think about the beautiful things you will own after you're successful. Imagine the people whose lives will be changed for the better once your success opens doors to their success. Think of why you had the dream in the first place and let nothing stop you from attaining it. When times get tough, recall why you started your journey. This will help you keep going, even when fear and doubt creep into your mind.

Step 5: Plan it.

Think of a way you can fund it and start working towards it. Set financial goals and start with your assets, family and friends. Research optional ways to obtain revenue. Plan short and long-term goals over the first 12 months of business. Put a budget in place for each of them and consider a part-time job if needed. It can also be done with a full-time job on the side utilizing time management skills to remain focused on the primary goal. Proper planning will help you avoid some of the pitfalls along the way.

Step 6: Build it.

Decide if you will start working out of your home or get office space beyond it. Think about a good marketing strategy and who you want to complete it. Complete an outline for a great website and the information that will display what your business is all about. Design business cards, logos, consider an EIN number, bank accounts and get phone and internet service ready. Secure funding and put a game plan in place for a grand opening.

Step 7: Protect it.

Be sure to remember insurance to protect the integrity of the business and your possessions. You must also protect yourself against negative press and reviews by making customer service a number one priority. Your brand shows who you are as a business; do not take this lightly. Attitudes within the company will also be necessary to keep in check. Staying positive and keeping negative energy to a minimum will be worth the effort.

Step 8: Enjoy it.

Once your success is achieved, remember to take time to appreciate the good times. Spend quality time with family and friends. Feel free to take vacations and buy new things. Balance is the key and should be a good gauge in everything that you accomplish. Consistently working and never taking a moment to enjoy the fruit of your labor is tragic. Appreciate your success and preserve it by understanding the need to make time for yourself!

·2·

What's Stopping You?

What's keeping you from fulfilling your dreams? Is it fear, lack of funding, not enough time, or not driven enough? Whatever is holding you back, you must overcome it. If you wait for the perfect time, you will never start. When you work for what's holding you back and learn to get real with yourself, you can begin to see your plan come to success. It all starts with you; you hold the key to unlocking your full potential. Stop wasting time!

1. Fear: If you have a fear of failing, you're not alone; however, you will need the courage to get beyond those thoughts. Fear can hold you captive from your destiny if you allow it. It's all in your state of mind. If you think you can't, you won't. When you refuse to believe, you can't achieve. The good news is, there are steps you can take to help you gain knowledge and confidence. You can start by visiting or reaching out to someone who has found success in your area of interest. They will have valuable insight and knowledge that can help you get beyond your anxieties. You can learn best practices and specific things to potentially avoid. Your entrepreneur spirit comes with many risks and rewards. The best in the business accepted the challenge and conquered their fears. You must know that you're worth all the tears, sweat and time it takes to make this new venture work. Embrace your fears, instead of avoiding them; use your mistakes to help you grow stronger. The wisdom you gain, as you tackle these obstacles, will be priceless. Once you get past the fear factor, there are no guarantees that your road will be successful. It's a chance you must be willing to take; conversely, doing nothing will never get you to where you want to be in life. Your passion, hard work, and belief in your ideas can help put you over the top. Silence the voice in your head that tells you what you can't accomplish and replace it with your voice, saying "I can conquer anything, nothing can hold me back." You must get beyond excuses, money issues, time restraints and become driven if you want to satisfy your taste for success.

2. Procrastination: Are you the person who says, I'll get to it tomorrow? I don't ever seem to have any extra money. I'm not sure if they will like what I offer. If this is familiar territory, you're full of excuses; you're all talk and no action! You can change that behavior today, by planning short and long-term goals, to get closer and closer to where you need to be. One of the first things you can do after setting your short-term goals is to set an immediate deadline date and share it with someone. It will give you the boost needed to begin your first phase. It will also make you feel obligated to complete your tasks because you're accountable to someone other than yourself. Your ability to execute your plans will prove that you're more than just talk, and one who can make things happen. Putting attainable goals in place will be necessary to push through the smoke of procrastination.

3. Time Management: Time is one of the more precious resources that we have available. Time lost can never be regained. If you are trying to find success, there will never be enough hours in the day to complete everything. You will always feel that there is more to do before you get started on any major goals. You can't sweat the small stuff. Instead, know that you have what it takes to make things happen. Jump in head first. It's scary, but can be incredibly rewarding.

4. Finances: Cash flow issues are usually the cause of businesses that fail before they have a real chance to flourish. It will be imperative to do your homework if you want to keep the doors open. The internet is a great tool to help you find alternative business funding if you're not qualified for traditional loans. Take the time to do meaningful research. Seek financial partners who can offer short-term working capital loans or alternatives to keep your business afloat. It should be at the top of the priority list as you put your plan into action.

5. Drive: It takes drive to take a dream from a thought to a successful product or service. It is also what keeps things going when times are tough. People who are driven never stop trying. Obstacles and barriers seem to be no match for them. One of the characteristics that winners have in common is drive. It can catapult you to the Power Chair if you are one of the lucky few to possess it.

If you want to sit in the Power Chair, you must make certain sacrifices. Investing in you will require time and commitment. It will not always be easy, but can be extremely rewarding. You are worth every minute that you spend putting the pieces together to move forward. If you can spend countless hours doing work for others, you can find time to contribute to your own goals. You can start laying the foundation for your legacy, instead of building someone else's dreams.

There are so many lost gifts and talents in the cemetery. Countless individuals who thought about owning a business, graduating from college or creating innovative products, only to sit on the sidelines until it was too late. Don't allow this to be your story. Act now. You have all the necessary tools to get this done. They have been right in front of you the entire time.

·3·

Believe in Yourself

One of the most significant hurdles to the Power Chair is lacking the confidence that you are equipped with the skills to get there. Many people think that "If you dream it, you can achieve it," is just a cliché. If you never dare to dream or become bold in your actions, it can seem like words alone. You can accept this fate, or you can take Nike's advice and "Just Do It." So many dreams are deferred or never revealed for various reasons. This doesn't have to define your aspirations; you should work daily on executing plans to fulfill your ambitions.

If you think about it, you have a thought or idea that has been tucked away in the back of your mind for some time. It's something that you recall at certain moments, but put minimal effort towards. Well, it's time to go beyond thoughts and research ways to make it a reality. You will need to be passionate about setting goals to achieve it. No one is going to give you a handout and that should come as no surprise. On the other hand, if you can find one right cheerleader to help keep your dream alive, it can

9

make a huge difference. Sometimes you need reassurance from someone else, one who believes in you and your capabilities. A constant or occasional nudge can be beneficial in many ways.

An excellent example of this practice is Angela Smith and her friend Regina Hall who have known one another for about seven years. Angela shared her dream of owning a company that helps start-up businesses with marketing, employee development, and website design. Angela also worked full-time for a local resort as a General Manager, working extremely long hours, to make the company successful. Each day that Angela spoke with Regina, she would ask, what's going on with the business that you're working on? Angela didn't have much to add because she was so busy with her career at the resort. She was exhausted after work and had no time to plan or think about her own goals. Her friend would say, "You're doing a great job at the resort, but when will you put time into your business plans?" It was uncomfortable for Angela, but a much-needed reminder of what was important to her. The weeks and months passed, but Regina continually asked the same question over and over, "Have you started planning yet?"

One day, Regina suggested that Angela take at least 30-45 minutes each day, to complete work on her personal goals of opening a business. Regina would continuously bounce around different suggestions that might help Angela begin her consulting company. It was this type of positive influence and cheerleading that gave Angela the strength to put time into her goals. Eventually, the conversation took a surprising turn. It was Angela calling to inform her friend that she was writing a business plan and putting ideas in place to achieve her lifelong dream. She also thanked her for being such a beautiful and caring friend. The lesson is, you will need to find someone similar and allow them to help keep your dream alive.

Who do you have in your corner? If you don't have anyone right now and you're procrastinating on your goals, get help now. There is value in a good friend or family member who can surround you with positive energy and new ideas to move your goals forward. You might want to do everything on your own, but please note, you can't do all facets of business by yourself. To share the workload with someone else leaves more time for you to focus on essential needs, to make the business run smoothly.

Erin Cummings has a great quote; "At the end of the day, you are solely responsible for your success and your failure. And the sooner you realize that, you accept that, and integrate that into your work ethic, you will start being successful. As long as you blame others for the reason you aren't where you want to be, you will always be a failure." It all begins and ends with you. The choice is yours, rise to the occasion, or sink below your expectations. You're capable of achieving anything you set your sights on, so get to it.

You will have people in your corner rooting for you and those who will try to bring you down. Don't waste time focusing on the negative influences. They should be motivation alone. Your time is precious, and there's none to waste. You are preparing for a new beginning, one of upward movement, and leaving the naysayers behind.

·4·

Let Your Haters Hate!

To sit comfortably in the Power Chair, you must possess thick skin. Many individuals will hurl insults, scour your reviews and try to make life hard for you. You will need to manage your thoughts and not fall victim and allow this to influence your plans. It might come as a shock to you, that family and friends might be some of the first critics of your achievements. There will be the ones who stand with you, and those who will champion your demise. No worries, keep your head up and march on. This is not a blanket, or a one size fits all statement. Some of them will celebrate and champion your rise to the top; it's important to prepare yourself either way.

It's easy, of course, for people to judge you on your glory, but difficult for them to understand your story. They may see your new homes, automobiles or other things that you possess; however, what they might be missing, is the long days and nights you spent working on your dream; or the countless times you tried to get funding to no avail. Perhaps they missed the days that you had doubt and wondered if you would ever make it. It doesn't matter in the end. Let your haters hate!

You must be willing to keep your head up high and move beyond what other people think of you. There will be no shortage of people to find fault. You shouldn't waste a lot of precious time worrying about what's being said about you. By the way, if they were busy trying to make their dreams come true, there would be no time left to worry about hating on you. It can be frustrating, but if you spend countless time on people who don't appreciate your accomplishments, it can derail you. Besides, what difference does it make? These individuals will never seek to pay your mortgage, automobile payments or any other obligations that you incur. This should add fuel to your inner energy tank and push you closer to the finish line.

The intelligent thing to do is to keep all negative people out of your immediate surroundings. It can make a huge difference in your success or failure. Negative people will only drag you down and cause headaches. It's impossible to count on them as a positive effect on what you're trying to accomplish. Honestly, you will never be able to please everyone all the time, and to put effort into trying, will be fruitless. Haters are apparently people who would be happy to celebrate any failures you might have rather than acknowledge your successes. The best thing for you is to ignore them and keep doing what you do best.

You can only control your actions and leave others to deal with their own. Stay focused on your most important objectives to clear your path forward. Having someone despise you can be used as motivation to push you to new levels of success. You can view it as a sign that you've made it when you have someone who envies your rise. Your goals are too big, too important and all-encompassing to allow haters to rain on your parade. You should spend minimal time answering or reading negative comments online. The things that can be of value will find its way to you. You will need your energy to spark new ideas, reinvest in your business and manage a great team. The more you starve your haters of attention; you might soon see them disappear. As Frank Sinatra has stated, "The Best Revenge is Massive Success."

·5·

Moral Ground

Values are important, and you must make sure that you possess a good moral compass. Many great people found success, only to later fall from grace. It's amazing how revealing the words, "power tends to corrupt and absolute power corrupts absolutely" can ring true. It's not the fate of all successful people; however, it's the road traveled for many individuals who never expected the downfall. Character and integrity must go into the power struggle as you rise to the top. It should be at the core of every man or woman who is fortunate enough to find success. Exposure to power, temptation and wealth can be a blessing and a curse. You will need to make sound decisions and try to avoid temptations that can cause grief for you and your family. It's not obtaining great wealth and success in life that's evil, and it's the love of them that's at the root of all evil. There are highs and lows associated with power and wealth. How you choose to navigate the potential obstacles can determine if you rise or fall.

Imagine being George Watkins, Vice President of Student Affairs at the university, and having great success showcasing why he was an asset to the school. He was an academic scholar and was influential in taking the department he headed into national acclaim due to his hard work and perseverance. The president of the university was stepping down due to conflict with the Board of Trustees. These conflicts were played out on the television for the entire world to see and were difficult to watch. The time came when the president decided that it was time to part ways and stepped down. This gave an opening for someone to fill in as the interim president until a permanent president could be selected.

A committee was formed, and the search began for a new president. In the meantime, the need for an interim president could not be understated due to the pressing needs of the university. After the Board met to discuss the next move, George Watkins was considered due to his academic background, knowledge of the university and the level of respect he had within the community. He was to step in and fill the gap until a new president could be named. One thing that George offered was a seamless transition when the new president was appointed. George was a humble man, intelligent and well equipped for the job at hand. He also offered the search committee a signed contract that he wouldn't become a candidate for president. He also assured the Board that being Vice President of Student Affairs was where his heart was, and the transition would be smooth.

George started his position as interim president and by all accounts was doing a great job in the first few weeks. He was interacting with the students, getting new staff in place and handling the affairs of the university with poise and great leadership.

He began to be showered with gifts, influential people were on his calendar, and he was making more money than ever before. This gave George a sense of pride, and he realized the feeling of sitting in the Power Chair. After all, he worked hard, made it against all the odds and was now at the top of his game. As the weeks passed by, the Board was vetting new presidential prospects and getting closer and closer to a final decision. George was enjoying being showered with more and more gifts, meeting famous people who visited the campus and receiving praise from the student body on a job well done.

He was at the best place in his life, but things were about to change. The committee was close to narrowing the candidates down to the final 3 and planning to present the new president. It was at this point that George began to think about the fantastic job that he was doing, the accolades that he received and how good it felt to be in the Power Chair. He reached out to the Board and requested a meeting to discuss where things stood. They were delighted to meet with him to discuss his thoughts so far and to go over the smooth transition that had been addressed in an earlier time in the process. To their surprise, George requested to be considered for the position and become the president on a permanent basis. The Board members were shocked! George had offered and signed an agreement that he wouldn't seek the position, and the Board didn't want any more public discourse.

George was relentless in the meeting explaining why he was best suited for the position. The Board members reminded George that he signed a binding contract and that he wouldn't be considered for the position. He couldn't believe that they didn't see things from his point of view. After all, he was doing a fantastic job and had the support of the student body. The Board would hear no more, and the meeting was adjourned. George was devastated and left to find a way to get around the contract to be named president of the university. He hired an Attorney; he made his desire for the position public and planned a march at the university with the support of many students. The need to keep this seat and newfound power superseded everything going on around him.

George called his best friend, Angela Smith, to meet for coffee and discuss what was going on in his life. They met and went over the details of the contract he signed. Angela asked him why he would cause uproar over a position that he only wanted temporarily. He stated that after becoming the interim president, it came with so many perks, he met so many talented people and it felt good to wield so much power. He fell victim to the success of the Power Chair and refused to give it up quickly. Going back to the previous position didn't seem attractive; besides, he made it to what appeared to be his destiny.

He planned his march and was followed by many students and individuals within the community. The news outlets captured the vast number of people who came out to support George. They gave their testimonies on why they thought he was equipped to run the university. The contract he signed seemed to be of no consequence to his followers. The community and student body were split on their feelings, and this caused discord throughout the city.

The Board didn't back down and named a new campus president. George was offered his previous position to his dismay. He decided to pass on the offer and left the university altogether. He researched new positions at other campuses in need of a president. He concluded his talents might be better utilized in a new state and where he could start over. After having a taste of power when he sat in the highest seat on campus, it was difficult to go back where he started.

George Watkins' story is a familiar one, and it comes with many twists and turns. There is something that's hard to explain to anyone who hasn't had the opportunity to sit in "The Power Chair." It can be a feeling of pride, authority, power, and accomplishment; a sense of being on top of the world. Once a person gets the chance to sit in the Power Chair, it becomes difficult to think of a better place to be. It comes with so much prestige, gifts and wealth. No one thinks about the pitfalls until they're falling in the ditch.

Pitfalls can be minimized and avoided if you are vigilant. Someone else's fate does not have to be yours. You have been building your character since you were young. When you're open and ready to make needed changes, you can. John Wooden wrote, "The true test of a man's character is what he does when no one is watching." In your private time, it's worth asking, "Who am I when no one is watching?" If you need to adjust, do it. You are not handcuffed to a past that you choose to modify unless you decide not to change.

·6·

Remember Where You Came From

The Power Chair has been filled with people who were once a part of the struggle in the workplace. It's important to remember how things started; it will keep you humble and help you resist having the Power Chair consume you. When you understand the situations you once faced, bringing awareness to those experiences can be constructive.

Even after finding success, remember the importance of being heard within the company and treating everyone fairly. After finally reaching your idea of success, don't forget the struggle. A word of advice; it might be helpful to be less removed from the people who are the engine of your dream. The people who work hard and need to be valued; people who can give innovative thoughts as you once did in the workplace.

Everyone will not fit into the vision or goals you have for your company. Some won't make it and will need to be let go; however, the majority will probably have the best interest of your business at heart. Investing in an excellent management team is a key responsibility. A manager who leads by example; one who exhibits the ability to measure and reward performance while understanding accountability for all.

Never find yourself in a position where you become the individual you loathed while you were in the trenches in the workplace. You're the boss now and your actions matter. When you worked for someone else, you had ideas, but they were rarely heard, no one in Management asked your opinion. Try to remember how this made you feel and have a more open door for ideas with people who work for you. It's easy to isolate the past and insulate yourself from where you came from; you have a choice. Keep your ear to the ground and make your employees feel valued.

Challenging your team to think is beneficial for everyone and is necessary if you want to grow. Keeping fresh ideas and thoughts will ensure forward progress when coupled with keeping complacency within the business at bay. Setting the bar high regarding expectations can help the company grow exponentially. It can also help stretch your employees and help them to understand what's expected daily. On the other hand, employees who are under constant threat of losing their job, have unrealistic goals to meet and are oppressed can't perform to their highest potential. This will not hold true for all employees, but it's worth a review.

When you start out seeking new business, you're usually full of excitement, vigor, and great expectations. You're gifted, and failure is not an option in your estimation. You see yourself one day owning one of the premier businesses in the world. It's hard to bottle your enthusiasm, and it's so refreshing to see the hard work pay off. You're waking up early and going to bed late; ideas are flowing, and you're putting the final pieces together after a long struggle to get started. What was once just a thought, is on its way to becoming all that you dreamed it to be and more. Having the right attitude is one of the intangibles that can make a difference.

True humbleness is one of the most valuable traits that an excellent leader exhibits. Don't mistake it for weakness. It's being supportive without being submissive.

·7·

Don't Let Your Passions Die

If you think the Power Chair is not in reach for you, think again. There is not a particular group of people who have a monopoly on great success. You could be the next success story. What are you doing now to make this a reality? Are you putting things off until a better day or waiting for the perfect time to act? Never allow procrastination or fear keep you from your dreams. Individuals who are successful, take risks that others are unwilling to take. They don't possess less fear, they refuse to allow fear to stop them. If you could speak with many of them, they could share multiple stories of failures along the way. Stop living your life worrying about failing, and have the guts to take a leap of faith. You're worth it!

Consider Cathy Washington, a budding florist, who always dreamed of opening her own shop. She read many books about it while visiting other successful florists in the area, to pick their brains on how they made it. Cathy was tenacious and always believed that she could beat the odds regardless of her lack of college education. She called her local Small Business Administration for guidance and scheduled to meet to discuss her business aspirations. She received help with the business plan, advice on funding as well as marketing techniques. Cathy's excitement was palpable, and she had no shortage of people telling her she could do it.

After months of preparation, she designed and purchased business cards, postcards, brochures and put together a website. She was unable to get a traditional bank loan due to lack of credit history and collateral. She relied on limited savings along with help from family and friends. She located the perfect place for her shop and made an offer. It was a month to month lease to start, and Cathy was ecstatic. She finally opened her doors, and after months of anticipation, her dream was fulfilled. On the first day, one customer visited the shop, but this didn't alarm her. The next few days and weeks passed, but there was limited traffic to the store and Cathy became a little uneasy.

She used her savings and most of the money from family and friends. Rent on the shop was coming due and additional bills were trickling in weekly. Cathy began to let doubt creep in and wondered if she should have started this journey. This is a real moment. It can happen to anyone when preparation for the good and bad days is not planned. Rainy days can find anyone in business, but it's not the end of the road, and things can turn around. Cathy decided to tweak things a bit and offer coupons and sales on specialized items. She got the word out through her website and social media platforms. This paid off, and she began to see an increase in customers online as well as in the shop. The activity continued to grow, and the business was in a better place.

There were many lessons learned to include the importance of having robust plans and funding in place for tough times. One of the other great experiences is being willing to change course and try something new to generate profits. Your initial idea might be great, but have no customers willing to invest in it. Find your niche and change directions to meet their needs. That's just smart business and can open the door to future growth in your business.

Cathy experienced doubt as many individuals who pursue new businesses will, but she continued to believe in herself and press forward. When you learn how to accept the good and bad days, you gain necessary insight and wisdom to make sound decisions, as problems arise. You learn that you are stronger than you thought, and the future doesn't seem so scary anymore. Fear can stifle some of the most influential minds in the world; you're not alone.

Often success or failure in business is all about perspective. How you decide to view a situation can determine the outcome. Many people think, "I haven't done anything with my life" or "I'm such a waste." Many other examples could be given to highlight the torture in one's mind regarding them. These thoughts can cause someone to look at their life and decide they have nothing to offer society. Confidence is an important element of them finding success.

A perfect example is Marsha Turner, a native of Cocoa Beach, FL. She is excellent in marketing, web design, writing and she's artistic to boot. She is the perfect example of a quadruple threat and an asset to most any company. Her creative abilities can take an obscure company from an unknown to the top if only she could believe in herself. With all these gifts, she can't seem to see her worth. The truth is, many people would love to possess even one of her gifts.

She met a few friends for coffee at a local shop to chat. They talked about their current careers and how it would be fun to get away for a girl's trip soon. As they began to chat, Marsha began to confide in them, sharing her innermost feelings. She spoke about a time in her life when she was at a low point. She shared that she didn't always believe in herself and thought she had been in a state of depression for months. Everyone at the table was shocked because they had a different perspective of Marsha and her accomplishments. In fact, she was the one most admired, because of her talents. She continued to share her experience and expressed how she recently found her voice by seeking help. After months of therapy, she is happy, healthy and ready to take on new challenges.

She informed her friends that she's moving to a new city to open a new life coaching business. She wants to give back to others and help anyone suffering from low self-esteem or anything holding them back from reaching their highest potential. She recently obtained her certification in life coaching and will utilize her experience in graphic design and marketing. Marsha's friends were happy for her and ready to celebrate all she had accomplished. Combatting depression and opening a business had them admiring her even more; they always viewed her as the one with the highest potential.

If you can change the way you view life's obstacles, tasks, and goals, it can aid you in overcoming many hurdles. These barriers can stand in the way of your professional and personal growth. On the other hand, thinking how the problem will overtake you is when failure can take root. It's all about perspective and believing that there is no situation you encounter, that is impossible for you to solve.

When you see yourself in a bad light and have low self-esteem, it can keep you from maximizing your full potential. On the road to success, if these issues are not resolved, it can keep you from fulfilling your dreams. It's imperative to have a positive perspective when dealing with life's hurdles. It can help you change the way you overcome stumbling blocks. When you use your most difficult moments as tools to gain strength-that's powerful. Your failures are not there to defeat you, but to help you gain perspective. It's all in how you perceive it.

·8·

Pitfalls to Avoid

To avoid the pitfalls of the Power Chair, one must remember to be humble. The ability to rise to the top is awesome and worthy to be celebrated. It's a wonderful accomplishment that many people aspire to duplicate. There are several ways to remain humble and stay above the fray. There are five pitfalls that can be identified; when one falls from the Power Chair, they are the usual suspects. You can be on the road to success or amid it, but these potential pitfalls should be avoided at all costs.

1. Arrogance: To be self-centered in business or your personal life will likely lead to disaster if it's not put in check. When you look at several successful executives who have fallen from grace, arrogance was a large part of the equation. There is nothing wrong with having confidence in yourself, but when self-importance defines you, it can be why you might unravel over time. One way to combat this is to remember your humble beginnings. Try to remember those who assisted you along the way and realize that it takes more than your hard work to make it.

2. Overindulgence: It can be drugs, alcohol, possessions or anything where there's unnecessary behavior, problems can follow. Less might be more in this instance and not worth losing what you gave time, sweat and tears to build. It can be lonely at the top, and where there is success, there is more responsibility as well. For some, this can lead to abuse of alcohol and drugs; or buying things that are well beyond what you can truly afford. To avoid these issues, remember to use them in moderation, if at all. Set a budget that is reasonable and stick to it. Set limits on your alcohol intake and commit to never starting any drugs. This can be a slippery slope, and any of these potential pitfalls are not worth losing what you've worked so hard to obtain.

3. Crisis Management: Knowing how to anticipate and manage problems can define great leaders. It is necessary to have problem-solving skills and the willingness to confront issues head-on with solutions that keep the integrity of the business intact. Whether the problem is big or small is of no consequence. They are all important to resolve. The smallest threat may be what dooms the business if left unchecked. Great leaders are not intimidated by problems that arise; instead, they are equipped with the capability of taking on difficult tasks and dealing with them promptly.

4. Poor Insight: You must be willing to say "no" to a deal even if it's lucrative, especially when it's illegal. You can't love money and possessions more than you love yourself or family. You must be careful about the company you keep, recognizing that a trusted few are best. Allow an Attorney to review all documents before you're willing to sign anything. One lawsuit or legal issue can derail everything, but careful planning and good legal advice can prevent unnecessary pitfalls. Avoid seeking the shortest and quickest route to making money. Nothing great ever comes easy, and as the saying goes "if it's too good to be true, it probably is." Get rich quick schemes are only a setback, a waste of precious time and resources. It's better to come up with a plan and execute a timeline to complete your goals.

5. Greed: Greed can bring an individual to their knees and threaten all that they've gained. It is one of the main culprits when you lose everything because you let possessions rule you. Greed comes in several forms and can lead to loss of business, worldly items or even loved ones. The decision is always met with a stark choice whether to do right or wrong. Making an incorrect choice can impact you, your family and friends in a negative way. The good news is that you can resist glutinous behavior, deciding to live within your means, opting to refrain from the wrong connections or giving in to the temptation of deals that you should walk away from immediately.

By no means are these five potential pitfalls the only ones to avoid; nor are they intended to cover all scenarios that you may face. They are important to keep in mind if you want to avoid disasters that can be in front of you. The list could cover so many additional pitfalls and a host of disasters that can befall anyone; what's more important is that your eyes and ears stay open to anything that can prevent you from falling victim. Don't hesitate to act when necessary and avoid anything that can cause harm. The Power Chair is yours for the taking if you're up for

35

the challenge. Being overly cautious or risky comes with ups and downs, you must choose your moves wisely.

·9·

Your Inner Circle

Who has your ear? It matters who you keep within your inner circle. When you make it to the top, the most influential people in your trusted group can have a negative or positive effect on your agenda. They must have your best interests at heart always. These individuals are the gatekeepers and assistant decision makers. If they don't have integrity and a stable moral core, it can be costly for you. The people closest to you do matter, whether it's good or bad. There are traits you must remove or distance from your inner circle.

One trait to be wary of is the business partner or friend who thinks you never do anything wrong. They seem to idolize you and offer no constructive criticism that can be beneficial. When the boss makes mistakes, they tend to make excuses and explain why everyone else is at fault. Their hype can be your enemy when it's time to make tough decisions. They offer few chances for you to improve and thus can be better served from a distance.

Gossipers are toxic to the inner circle for various reasons. They suck the lifeblood from all whom they encounter; leaving innovation and thought-provoking topics on the sidelines. They seem to revel in the new juicy story of the day. Be careful what you share with them because it can be revealed to anyone who will listen. Minimizing contact or cutting them completely out of your life and business may be best.

The strife seeker within the inner circle keeps up turmoil. It's like having a devil on your shoulder. They are usually quite manipulative and cause unrest for everyone. When they have the bosses' ear, they can wreak havoc on the entire team. They are often found saying one thing to the boss and another thing to you, causing problems for all parties involved. They have no issue with sabotaging others to protect themselves. This type of behavior can be a cancer to the team and should be dismissed immediately if they don't change. Conversely, having someone with whom you can trust and bring about positive change is a blessing. When you have this person on board, take good care of them. Appreciate what they bring to the table. Gratitude goes a long way.

·10·

Work Hard and Take Care of Your Business

The Power Chair is yours for the taking; if you can find the strength to work hard for it. It's the feeling that a select few obtain while others can only dream and wonder what it feels like to own it. You can usually find common traits among most successful people; they include being assertive, cautious, intellectual, and ambitious. These are only a few examples, but are some of the best ways to describe the most brilliant business leaders. Bill Gates, Steve Jobs, Oprah Winfrey and Warren Buffet are some of the wealthiest individuals, and no doubt possess all or some of these traits. They don't have a monopoly on them; your name can be added to the list someday. Are you up for the challenge?

Do you have a product or service to solve a problem in your community or society? It can be big or small, but the time to come forward is now. You are potentially holding a great solution to a problem, and the world is waiting for you to reveal it. Anything standing in your path should be removed. You have too much to offer to continue to sit on the sidelines.

Vince Lombardi said it best; "The price of success is hard work, dedication to the job at hand, and the determination that whether we win or lose, we have applied the best of ourselves to the task at hand." These are great words of wisdom, and you should locate your favorite quote to read when times get tough. Inspiration can pick you up when you have no one to vent your innermost frustrations. There are no silver bullets when seeking success. You should find what works best for you. Your value system, positive mindset, and resources can be a good starting point to build upon. Be confident to take care of the things that matter most within the business. This includes financial health, customer needs, employee relations and your wellbeing.

If there is one area, where your business should not struggle, it's delivering exceptional customer service to those who fuel the company daily. Start-up businesses can go from obscurity to a booming entity by retaining a happy client base through extraordinary customer service. Not every business is concerned with making all customers happy, and it becomes detrimental to the survival of the company. You can have the best products, great business hours and a team in place; however, if you have no customers, you have no business.

Many resources, time and money are put into generating happy customers; when these customers are happy, they tend to tell others about your products and services. This can lead to repeat business and loyal customers for years to come. There are many ways to retain your current shoppers. You can greet each customer upon arrival, answer any questions that they may have and offer deals and customer feedback options, to name a few.

When you get a loyal customer, it is helpful to advertise their testimonials, allowing other people to want to visit as well. Be sure to make it easy for customers to find your products, locate your business and have easy returns or exchanges. This will not cover all aspects of your customers' needs, but it's a guideline to start gaining their trust.

The most successful businesses have customers feeling that they received more than they expected. Upon arrival, they are greeted by team members with smiles and every interaction throughout their visit is met the same from all employees. This is a culture that is manifested through proper training and effort from great leadership.

Customers tend to remember they're bad experiences more than the good ones. The impact of word of mouth to family and friends they encounter can be harmful. The use of online platforms to express their disgust exacerbates these issues even further. For these reasons, it is important to keep bad experiences to a minimum, if not completely avoided.

·11·

The Power of You

I want to share 14 powerful things to think about while you're seeking success in different areas of your life.

1. Do you ever wonder why the excitement of working towards your goal feels better than when you achieve it? Neuroscience reveals that the key to satisfaction is on the goals that we seek, rather than those we accomplish. You hear many stories about people who have created great wealth or won the lottery and are still not happy. It shows that acquiring these things do not correlate to long-term happiness. Many individuals who are seeking to win the lottery or become successful will do almost anything to have it. On the other hand, there are many wealthy people, who would trade what they have, to lead a life of pure peace and happiness. Peace of mind can't be purchased for any amount of money in the world, and it's priceless.

2. We are what we think. If you find yourself thinking that you will never be successful, you probably won't. If you envision yourself accomplishing your goals, you probably will.

Your movement to do the things that are important starts with what you think. It's important to allow positive energy to locate you, by putting it out into the universe yourself. Begin to write the things that you want to achieve; take 10 minutes each day to write or recite it. You will be surprised how the great things you seek become your new reality. The reverse is true as well, so spend time in positive thoughts, rather than negative ones.

3. Having a victim mentality is doing you a disservice. You are equipped with all the tools you need to become whatever you aspire to be. No one is promising that the road will be easy, but feeling sorry for yourself and blaming others, is not a recipe for success. Free your mind to explore new territory. Allow yourself to gain new insights, find your passion, and start doing at least one thing to make it happen.

4. Be grateful. If you are not a person who takes time to appreciate the small things in life, start today. Learn to be grateful for any and everything that happens in your life. Even in failure and loss, there are things to gain and give thanks. You will begin to starve your failures of oxygen and give life to those things that are the most important. It will be a spiritual awakening, and it will set you free. Believe it or not, there are no self-made successful men or women, regardless of what they tell you. It took someone to help them along the way; the same will be true for you.

5. How you feel about and view yourself is extremely important. Think big and beyond your current capabilities. Tell yourself each day, that there is no skill set that will keep you from your achievements. Surround yourself with people who are more successful and driven than you. This environment will stretch you and your abilities beyond your wildest dreams. It will only cause you to learn and grow in ways you might otherwise take for granted. You don't need to duplicate them; you're not a clone, but your successful design.

6. Acquiring wealth or possessions is not a sin. You should aspire to get everything that you feel you deserve and more. It takes money to pay the bills, eat or live comfortably. It's great when you can have the finer things in life. There is one caveat; never let these things own you, you should own them. You have worked hard for the things you have. Guilt and shame should not enter your mind, and you deserve it all; however, if you have lost your soul to gain this whole world, make a change right now. You're still breathing. It's never too late.

7. Be open. Capture the imagination of those whom you have the answer to their basic needs. Do not keep your gifts and talents bottled inside. Share your thoughts, products or time with people who can use it to their advantage. Leave your legacy for generations to come. You were born to do great things, what are you waiting on?

8. Leave any selfishness behind you. The more you give, the more you grow. In fact, giving is your secret weapon to advancing beyond your capabilities. It attracts people who want to give to you, and it will pay dividends for years and years. It's easier to build great teams with members who will give their best work to you when you gain their respect. Selfish people rarely understand this concept; they're too busy taking. Reciprocity is a foreign term. Expand your mind beyond just you because you will eventually need someone financially, emotionally or socially, to be there for you. Don't blow it, ditch the inner voice of selfish stupidity. You can offer so much more.

9. Allow failure to be your pathway to success. It's hard to swallow, but failure can lead to your best work and innovation. It's through mistakes that you earn your stripes. When things come easy, they usually go away just as easy. When you put in the time, effort, sweat and tears to build something, you gain perspective; you learn how to fight and keep what you built. Johnny Cash noted this great quote, "You build on failure. You use it as a stepping stone. Close the door on the past. You don't try to forget the mistakes, but you don't dwell on it. You don't let it have any of your energy, or any of your time, or any of your space." It's one of the greatest lessons that you can learn. As you begin to use your life experiences to move to the top, you will gain valuable insight along the way. Success isn't an overnight phenomenon; it takes time. Successful people are aware of the time it takes, that failure is inevitable, and sacrifices are all a part of the plan.

10. Live freely. One if the most important things that you can do when it's all said and done, is to free yourself. Learn to take advantage of what you should offer, and put it out to the world, on your terms. Don't get caught up in how many people you might offend or who will accept you as you strike out. Stay creative, open minded, unique, and know that there is room for you. You won't have to repackage someone else's work or hold off on breaking out because your work is not good enough. That's small-minded thinking.

11. You hold the key. So many people search all over the place for the answer to their dreams or solutions to their problems. The great news is, the answer is right in front of you. Start using the tools, resources, and knowledge that's around and within you. The door to your success isn't hidden from you. It's not a complicated maze or puzzle with missing pieces to keep you from completing it. You have all the pieces in your possession. You just need to take the time to put them together. Unlock the door to your dreams, and you will discover that you had the key, all along.

12. Nothing and no one is perfect. Are you a prisoner to perfection? If so, let it go. The need to get things right is good, but seeking perfection can be a stumbling block in your way. We all want to be satisfied and put forth our best work and creation; striving for perfection is an elusive feat. We are offered words of wisdom to help us move on by freeing our minds concerning perfection. "Perfection is impossible except in scientific laboratory experiments and mathematical applications. Most of the time, emphasizing perfection rather than excellence acts as an obstacle to progress." By M.S. Rao, Ph.D.

13. Learn respect. Have you stepped on anyone to get to the top? If so, I hope you want or have made peace with them. Upon self-reflection, I hope you realized that life is a circle and one day you may have to contend with the harm you caused. If this is your approach to success, rethink the strategy. Negative energy attracts negativity, and this may be the start of your path to things sabotaging your future as you hurt other people. It doesn't matter if you make yourself believe that the intentions were pure;

deep down, you are aware of the truth. It's probably time for you to do soul searching and make changes within. Perhaps you have no remorse and feel that you were in survival mode. If so, you're kidding yourself, and life will one day catch up to you.

14. Be honest and trustworthy. Trust is a major factor in all relationships. When it's broken with these tactics, it's almost impossible to regain. Ambition can make individuals see the reward ahead instead of the immediate pain of their actions when they pull these stunts. Whatever makes you do it, take time to find a cure for this pressing problem. It might help you get to the Power Chair, but you will hardly stay there. Make wise choices because the illusion of what you accomplished by stepping on others, will not lead to satisfaction for long. Cherish relationships with others over your drive for success at any cost. The price in the long run might be too much for you to pay. Think about it.

Enough reading about what, when and how you can be successful; it's time to get started. Whether you write a book, open a new business, finish college or solve one of the big problems in society, do it now! Try to complete a dream that seems beyond your wildest dreams or current capabilities. You may be surprised that people who know you well will not be shocked at all. Perhaps, the only person fighting your goals is You.

Measure success by your standards and live with the consequences of the outcome. It can be for better or worse, but it will be the picture that you painted. Let your life be a canvas that you paint with the colors that satisfy your insatiable appetite for success. It doesn't hurt to listen to the beat of your drum. There are so many ways to view success, you must find yours.

Get comfortable in your skin, build your confidence and stop waiting for the big break to find you. You can design a new set of rules, and though it might not be accepted in the beginning, it was a revolutionary idea. Most of the great things that we take for granted were thoughts ahead of their time and not always welcomed with open arms. Time is a precious commodity, don't waste another minute. Today is your day, and the Power Chair is waiting for you. It's time to decide today; there is no more time to waste, what's stopping you?

Bibliography

Cash, Johnny – "You build on failure...", from Academy of Achievement Interview June 25th, 1993, published on 20th Century Time Machine, YouTube (8/13/2016)

Cummings, Erin. – "At the end of the day...", from Backstage Interview by Shelley Brown 6 Tips from 'Harbor's Erin Cummings on Learning Acting Self Discipline (12/2/2013)

Dahlberg, John Emerich Edward – "Power tends to corrupt and absolute power...", from Lord Acton - Letter to Archbishop Mandell Creighton (April 5th, 1887)

Lombardi, Vince – "The price of success...", from article in http://www.yaseendadabhay.com/blog, *The Price of Success is Hard Work* by Yaseen Dadabhay (01/16/2015)

Nike "Just Do It" slogan, www.nike.com

Rao, M.S. PH.D. – "Perfection is impossible...", from article *Strive for Excellence, Not Perfection* by M.S. Rao, PH.D. in Training Magazine (11/03/2015)

Sinatra, Frank. – "The best revenge is massive success." http://theinspirationengine.blogspot.com/au/2012/best-revenge-is-massive-success.html, posted February 2012

Wooden, John. – "The true test of a man's character..."
http://www.huffingtonpost.com/the-blog/ posted January 2016

About the Author

Derilyn Sparrow, founder of *Breakthroughs8*, partners with entrepreneurs to enrich growth, innovation and development in their new business endeavors.

Derilyn attended *Florida A&M University* and graduated with a *B.A. Degree in Psychology* and *Masters Degree in Criminology*.

Derilyn speaks regularly to high school students, church congregations and employers on various topics. She also enjoys reading and reciting poems.

You can read more about Derilyn at her website:

www.breakthroughs8.org

www.ingramcontent.com/pod-product-compliance
Lightning Source LLC
Chambersburg PA
CBHW030035230526
45472CB00002B/522